THE HOFFNUNG
SYMPHONY ORCHESTRA

The Hoffnung Symphony Orchestra

by

Gerard Hoffnung

London: Dennis Dobson

First Published March 1955
Second Impression June 1955
Third Impression (revised edition) November 1955

I would like to express my thanks to Messrs.
Bradbury, Agnew & Co., Ltd., proprietors of
PUNCH, and to Hulton Press Ltd., for publishing
in advance some of the drawings in this book. GH

Published in Great Britain in 1955 *by Dobson Books Ltd.*
50 *Kensington Church Street, London, W.*8

Printed by Charles Pearson & Son Ltd., London

THE STRINGS

The Violin (Leader)

The Violon Double

The Viola

9

The Viola Pizzicato

The Yo-Bow

The Cello

The Double Bass (a left handed player)

13

The Piccolo Double Bass

The Harp

The String Tuba

This instrument is sometimes referred to as the "Minstrel Tuba" or the "Blow-Plucker". It is interesting to note that the String Tuba is a member of both the string and brass families though it is usually seated with the former.

The Zither

The Piano (Boudoir Grand)

18

The Spanish Guitar

The Ondes Martenot

20

THE WOODWIND

The Flute and the Piccolo Flute

The Bass Flute

The Oboe

26

The Cor Anglais

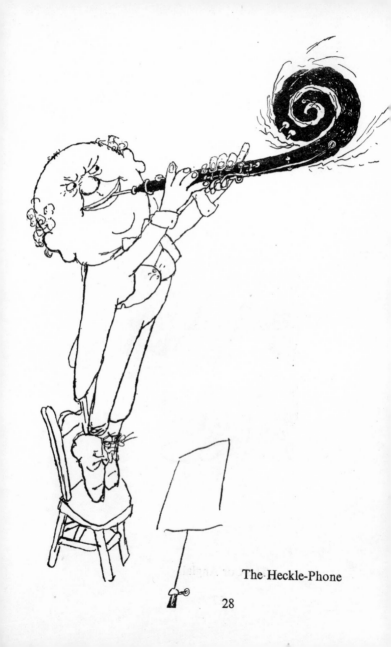

The Heckle-Phone

The Clarinet and the Bass Clarinet

The Saxophone

The Bassethorn

The Bassoon

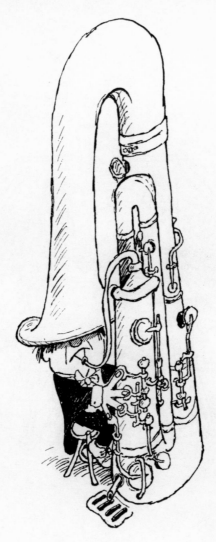

The Contra-Bassoon

33

The Organ

THE BRASS

The Horn

The Trinkler

The Double Trumpet

The Serpent

For security reasons this instrument
is no longer in use.

The Trombone

41

The Bass Trombone

The Wagner Tuba

The Bass Tuba

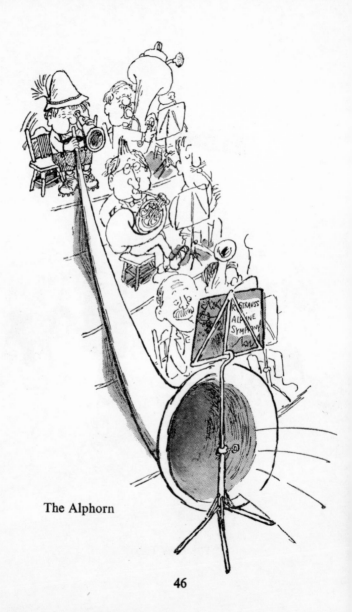

The Alphorn

THE PERCUSSION

THE DEPRESSION

The Timpani

The Cymbals

The Side Drum

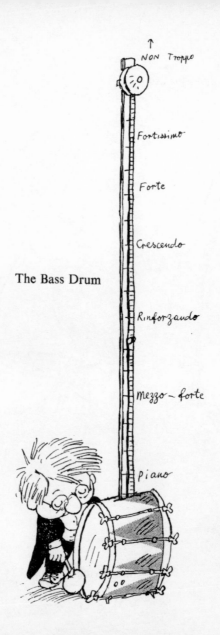

The Bass Drum

The Tum Drum

53

The Tubular Bells

The Triangle

55

The Xylophone

The Vibraphone

The Celeste

The Jingle Bells and the Chinese Block

The Wind Machine

The Gong and the Tam Tam

The Castanets

THE
END.

INDEX